NATIONAL GEOGRAPHIC

Missoula, Montana

COMMUNITIES AND THEIR LOCATIONS

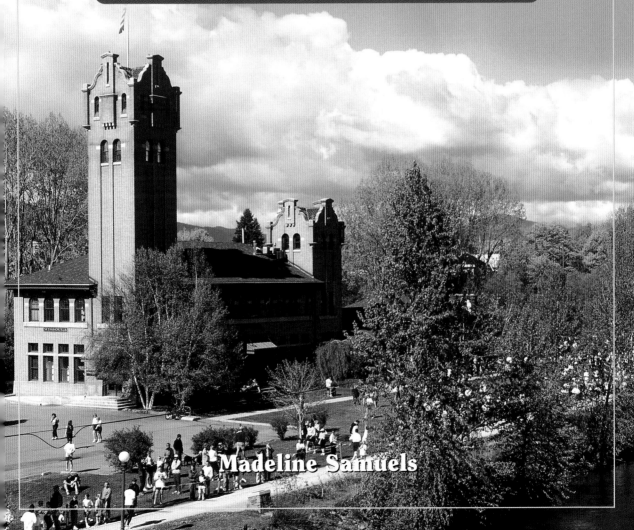

Madeline Samuels

PICTURE CREDITS
Cover: Missoula Valley with Lolo Peak in the background
© kenterphotography.com.

page 1 © kenterphotography.com; page 4 (bottom left)
© kenterphotography.com; page 4 (bottom right) © Mark E.
Gibson/Corbis/Tranz; page 5 (top) © kenterphotography.com;
page 5 (bottom left), Corbis; page 5 (bottom right), Honolulu
sunset © courtesy of Chuck Painter/HVCB; page 6, 8
© kenterphotography.com; pages 9–12, Corbis; pages 13–16
© kenterphotography.com; page 21 © John and Lisa Merrill/
Corbis/Tranz; page 23 © Jan Butchofsky-Houser/Corbis/Tranz;
page 24 © Joel W. Rogers/Corbis/Tranz; page 25 © Jan
Butchofsky-Houser/Corbis/Tranz; page 26 © kenterphotography.
com; page 29 © Mary Kate Denny/Stone/Getty Images;
background border, Magnolias on Commonwealth Avenue, Back
Bay, Boston © courtesy of FayFoto/Greater Boston Convention &
Visitors Bureau/BostonUSA.com.

Produced through the worldwide resources of the National
Geographic Society, John M. Fahey, Jr., President and Chief
Executive Officer; Gilbert M. Grosvenor, Chairman of the Board;
Nina D. Hoffman, Executive Vice President and President, Books
and Education Publishing Group.

PREPARED BY NATIONAL GEOGRAPHIC SCHOOL PUBLISHING
Ericka Markman, Senior Vice President and President, Children's
Books and Education Publishing Group; Steve Mico, Vice President
and Editorial Director; Marianne Hiland, Executive Editor; Richard
Easby, Editorial Manager; Jim Hiscott, Design Manager; Kristin
Hanneman, Illustrations Manager; Matt Wascavage, Manager of
Publishing Services; Sean Philpotts, Production Manager.

EDITORIAL MANAGEMENT
Morrison BookWorks, LLC

PROGRAM CONSULTANTS
Dr. Shirley V. Dickson, Program Director, Literacy, Education
Commission of the States; Margit E. McGuire, Ph.D., Professor of
Teacher Education and Social Studies, Seattle University.

National Geographic Theme Sets program developed by Macmillan
Education Australia, Pty Limited.

Published by the National Geographic Society
1145 17th Street, N.W.
Washington, D.C. 20036-4688

ISBN: 0-7922-4758-2

Product 41998

Printed in Hong Kong.

2008 2007 2006 2005
1 2 3 4 5 6 7 8 9 10 11 12 13 14 15

Contents

Communities and Their Locations

Think about the location of your community. Is it in the mountains or near the ocean? Is it on an island or close to a forest or river? The location of a community affects the lives of the people who live there. Missoula, Boston, St. Louis, and Honolulu are four communities in the United States with very different locations.

 Key Concepts ....

1. The location of a community has an effect on its economy and can help a community grow.

2. Location influences a community's way of life.

3. Over time, communities change in some ways and stay the same in others.

Four Communities and Their Locations

Missoula

Missoula, Montana is located near the Rocky Mountains.

Boston

Boston, Massachusetts is located along the Atlantic coast.

4

In this book you will learn about the mountain community of Missoula, Montana.

St. Louis

St. Louis, Missouri is located on the Mississippi River.

Honolulu

Honolulu, Hawaii is located on an island in the Pacific Ocean.

Missoula, Montana
A Mountain Community

Have you ever been to the mountains? You might have skied in the mountains in winter. You might have hiked in the mountains in summer.

Missoula is a mountain city. It lies near the center of five valleys in the Rocky Mountains. The mountains are very important to the people of Missoula.

A City in Montana

Missoula is in the state of Montana. Montana is in the western part of the United States. Missoula is one of the largest cities in Montana. Nearly 60,000 people live there.

The Rocky Mountains surround the city of Missoula.

Missoula was founded in the 1860s. Before then, the area was home to Native Americans. Native Americans often traveled through the valleys where Missoula now lies.

Look at the map. Find Missoula in the state of Montana.

Missoula Location Map

WASHINGTON

● Missoula

MONTANA

NORTH DAKOTA

OREGON

SOUTH DAKOTA

IDAHO

WYOMING

NEVADA

UTAH

N
W — E
S

0 mi.   200

0 km   200

United States

Key Concept 1 The location of a community has an effect on its economy and can help a community grow.

How Missoula Grew

A **community** is a group of people living together in one place. The location of a community affects how people earn a living.

community
a group of people living in an area

Missoula is located near forest-covered mountains. The soil in the region is very **fertile**. Both the forests and soil are important to Missoula's **economy**. The economy is the money that the community makes from its **businesses**.

economy
the wealth that a community gets from its businesses

Green forests and fertile soil helped the community of Missoula grow.

The First Business

The first business in the Missoula area was a **trading post**. The trading post was opened in 1860. It was built out of logs from nearby trees. The post sold supplies to travelers.

The business did well because of its location. People traveled through the area to cross the mountains.

Soon, there were **settlements** around Missoula. People came to farm in the fertile soil and cut trees for wood.

Logging in Montana was important for many years. These men are loading logs in the 1940s.

Missoula's Mills

The new settlers began to set up new businesses. Two mills were built in 1864. One mill was a sawmill. The local forests provided many trees for the sawmill. The other mill was a flour mill. This mill made flour from grains grown in the rich soil around Missoula. More settlers came to work in the mills. Soon other businesses were started. The economy grew.

Stores, schools, and hospitals opened. Missoula continued to grow.

The railroad helped transport logs across Montana.

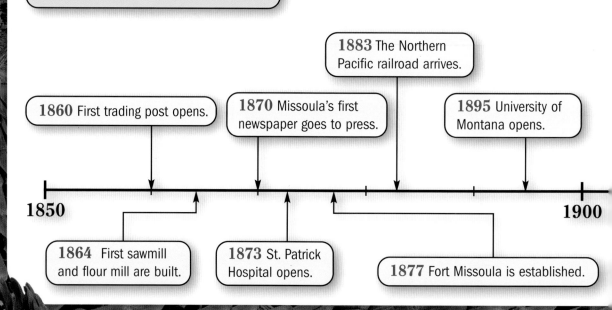

Timeline of Missoula's History

1883 The Northern Pacific railroad arrives.

1860 First trading post opens.

1870 Missoula's first newspaper goes to press.

1895 University of Montana opens.

1850

1900

1864 First sawmill and flour mill are built.

1873 St. Patrick Hospital opens.

1877 Fort Missoula is established.

The First Railroad

In 1883, the railroad arrived in Missoula. The railroad builders came to Missoula because its businesses were growing. The new railroad helped businesses in Missoula. They could now send goods to other parts of the country. The railroad also brought new goods to the people of Missoula.

The Pulp Mill

In 1956, Missoula opened its first pulp mill. A pulp mill makes paper out of wood. Selling paper made from local trees made a great amount of money for Missoula's economy.

Evans Avenue, a main road in Missoula, in 1941

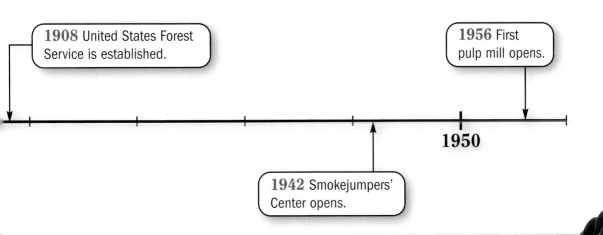

1908 United States Forest Service is established.

1956 First pulp mill opens.

1950

1942 Smokejumpers' Center opens.

Key Concept 2 Location influences
a community's way of life.

Life in Missoula

Missoula lies in the Rocky Mountains. The city is 3,200 feet (975 meters) above sea level. The location influences the way people in the area live, or their way of life. The plants and animals of the region once gave food and shelter to Native Americans. Today, the mountains and valleys around Missoula provide jobs and activities.

A Native American camp near Missoula

Jobs

The mountains around Missoula have thick forests. Many people in Missoula have jobs related to these forests. Some are outdoor jobs with the United States Forest Service. Forest Service workers take care of the forests. They also make sure people follow rules when they hunt animals in the forest.

There are still many mill jobs in Missoula. Some people work in the sawmills. They turn trees from the forests into wood for building. Some people work at the pulp mills. They turn wood into paper.

Recreation

The mountains around Missoula are ideal for **recreation**. During the winter, the mountains are covered in snow. People ski and snowboard on the mountains. The mountains are fun in the summer, too. People can ride bicycles, hike, and fish in the rivers.

A cyclist crossing a bridge in Missoula

Tourism

Tourism also affects the way people in Missoula live. Many visitors, or tourists, come to Missoula in both summer and winter. They come to enjoy the outdoor activities.

Tourism brings jobs to the people of Missoula. Many people have opened hotels, stores, and restaurants. Other people have set up tours. Some people work as guides to show tourists Missoula's attractions.

In winter, tourists come to Missoula to enjoy snow sports on the slopes of the Rocky Mountains.

Key Concept 3 Over time, communities change in some ways and stay the same in others.

The City Over Time

All communities grow and change. New families come to live in a community. New buildings are built. Most communities, though, keep important parts of their past.

Population

Missoula's **population**, or the people living there, has changed over time. Once, only Native Americans lived in the area. They depended on the forests and wildlife for food and shelter. When European settlers came, life in Missoula changed. People set up factories. Railroads cut across the mountains. The settlers built dams and bridges across Missoula's rivers.

Today, nearly 94 percent of people in Missoula are white. Only around 1,350 people are Native Americans.

The people of Missoula at a community event

Buildings

The buildings in Missoula are a mix of new and old. The new buildings show that Missoula is a modern city with a strong economy.

Older buildings stand among Missoula's newer buildings. Fort Missoula was built as a military post for the army in 1877. Today it is used as a museum. Older buildings like the fort show that the people of Missoula are proud of their past.

Downtown Missoula is a mix of new and old buildings.

Think About the Key Concepts

Think about what you read. Think about the pictures and the map. Use these to answer the questions. Share what you think with others.

1. Give two or more facts about the location of this community.

2. In the early days, how did the community's location help it to grow?

3. Give two or more facts about the way of life in this community today.

4. How has this community changed over time? How has it stayed the same?

VISUAL LITERACY

Political Map

Political maps show the locations of countries, states, towns, and cities.

Political maps show the borders of countries and states. They also mark the locations of towns and cities. Many political maps also label natural features, such as mountains, rivers, and deserts.

Different things can be shown on a political map.

Look back at the map on page 7. It is a political map that shows the location of Montana and Missoula in the United States. The map on page 19 is also a political map. It shows the state of Montana and some of its towns, cities, and natural features.

How to Read a Political Map

1. **Read the title to learn what the map shows.**
   Political maps can show the whole world, a continent, a country, a state, or just a city.

2. **Read the key to learn what the symbols stand for.**
   The key identifies the different symbols used on the map.

3. **Study the scale.**
   The scale shows you the size of the distances shown on the map.

4. **Think about what you have learned.**
   What new information did you learn about the place shown on the map?

Political Map of Montana

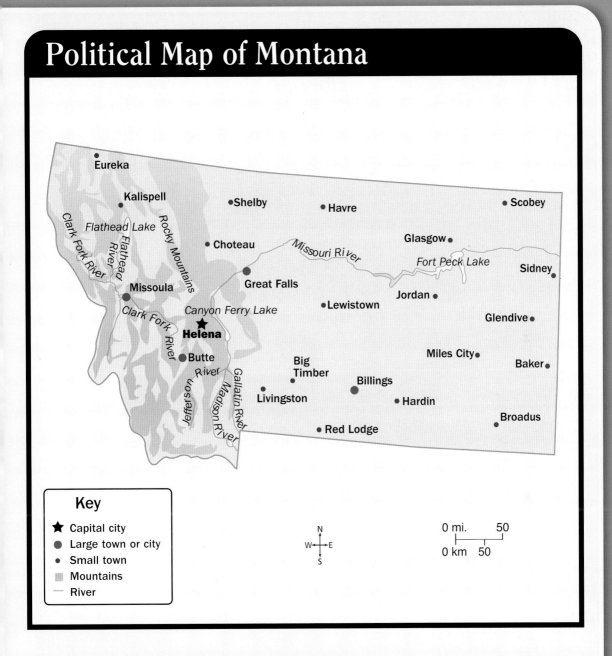

Eureka

Kalispell

Shelby

Havre

Scobey

Flathead Lake

Rocky Mountains

Glasgow

Clark Fork River

Flathead River

Choteau

Missouri River

Fort Peck Lake

Sidney

Great Falls

Missoula

Jordan

Clark Fork River

Canyon Ferry Lake

Lewistown

Glendive

★ **Helena**

Butte

Jefferson River

Madison River

Gallatin River

Big Timber

Miles City

Baker

Billings

Livingston

Hardin

Broadus

Red Lodge

Key

★ Capital city
● Large town or city
• Small town
▦ Mountains
— River

N
W—E
S

0 mi.   50

0 km   50

What's on the Map?

Read the map by following the steps on page 18. Answer the following questions. Where is Missoula located in Montana? What kinds of natural features are near the city? How many large towns or cities are shown on the map? What is the capital city of Montana?

Travel Brochure

Travel brochures give facts about a place that will be useful to a visitor. They describe interesting sights in order to persuade the reader to visit the place. The brochure starting on page 21 describes Missoula.

Travel brochures generally include the following:

Teaser
The teaser is a type of headline intended to capture the reader's attention.

Introduction
The introduction gives a general picture of the place.

Tourist Map
The tourist map shows the major tourist attractions and main streets.

Body Text
The body text has facts and descriptive details about the place. They are presented in a way that will make the reader want to visit.

Vacation in Missoula

The **title** names the place described in the brochure.

The **teaser** captures the reader's attention.

If you like to ski, hike, and enjoy wonderful scenery, then Missoula is the vacation place for you.

The **introduction** gives a general picture of the place.

About Missoula

Missoula lies in the beautiful Bitterroot Valley in Montana. It is surrounded by the Rocky Mountains. Thousands of acres of forests cover the mountains. The Clark Fork, Bitterroot, and Blackfoot rivers run through the valley.

Missoula is often called the "Garden City" because of its scenic location. The valley and the mountains offer many outdoor activities. Missoula also has a variety of cultural activities. Visitors come to see Missoula's theater and shopping centers. They also come to visit its museums and restaurants.

Getting Around

The best way to get around the city of Missoula is by car. You can rent a car at the airport or downtown. An excellent bus service operates in the downtown area.

Airport–Downtown

The Missoula International Airport is only five minutes from downtown Missoula. The taxi fare to the city center is not expensive. You could also be picked up by a shuttle service.

Where to Stay

Downtown Missoula lies on the banks of the Clark Fork River. The downtown area is a handy, central place to stay. Many pleasant hotels offer beautiful views.

Tourist Map of Missoula

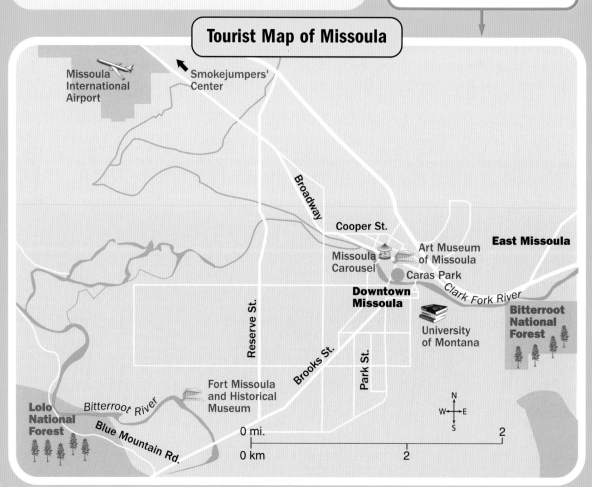

Missoula International Airport

Smokejumpers' Center

Broadway

Cooper St.

Missoula Carousel

Art Museum of Missoula

Caras Park

East Missoula

Downtown Missoula

Clark Fork River

University of Montana

Bitterroot National Forest

Reserve St.

Brooks St.

Park St.

Fort Missoula and Historical Museum

Bitterroot River

Lolo National Forest

Blue Mountain Rd.

N
W — E
S

0 mi.   2

0 km   2

Climate

Missoula has cold winters, with an average temperature of 26° Fahrenheit (-3° Celsius). The city receives about 50 inches (127 centimeters) of snow a year. The nearby mountains are a skier's paradise.

Summer temperatures average a comfortable 65° Fahrenheit (18° Celsius). Summertime is great for hiking.

What to See and Do

There is something for almost everyone in Missoula. Besides outdoor activities, there are also cultural places and events.

Smokejumpers' Center
The Smokejumpers' Center is the nation's largest smokejumping training base. Smokejumpers are people who protect forests from wildfires. They use parachutes to enter hard-to-reach areas to put out fires. You can take a guided tour of the training center.

Missoula Carousel
Take a ride on the hand-carved Missoula Carousel. The ponies and seats are beautiful. Volunteers from the community spent over 100,000 hours making the carousel.

Photographs support the information in the text.

Missoula Carousel is a favorite with children.

Sports Activities

River Rafting in Alberton Gorge

Rafting on the Clark Fork River through the gorge is fun and exciting. There are large cliffs along the river. You could see eagles, kingfishers, and hawks while rafting. You may also spot deer, moose, elk, and bears.

Hiking

Paths for walking and biking line the Clark Fork River's banks. Hiking trails are all around Missoula. You can follow trails in the Rattlesnake National Recreation Area, which is north of the city. The Sapphire Mountains also have many trails. The mountains are south of Missoula. Along the trails, you will find clear mountain lakes and beautiful waterfalls.

Skiing

There are two main ski areas close to Missoula – Montana Snowbowl and Marshall Mountain Ski Area. The Snowbowl is 30 minutes north of Missoula. Marshall Mountain Ski Area is just 7 miles (11 kilometers) northeast.

Skiing near Missoula

Recommended Tour

Fort Missoula and Historical Museum Tour

Do you want to find out about Missoula's history? Guided tours take you around Fort Missoula, which was established in 1877. You can walk around the Historical Museum. You can see cabins and other old buildings.

On site are a one-room schoolhouse and a United States Forest Service lookout. You can find out about the local Native Americans. You can also learn about Lewis and Clark, the early explorers of the area.

Wagon and log cabin exhibits at
Fort Missoula Historical Museum

Festivals

You can have fun in Missoula throughout the year. Here are some interesting festivals held in the city.

Downtown ToNight at Caras Park: June–September

Downtown ToNight in Caras Park offers live entertainment, food, and beverages each Thursday evening in the summer.

Fourth of July Celebration at Fort Missoula: July

The Fourth of July Celebration at Fort Missoula Historical Museum is held every year. Entertainment events and children's games are organized at the fort. Food and beverage stalls are also open during the celebration.

KidsFest: July

The KidsFest is held at Caras Park. It has games, contests, stage performances, dancing, music, and craft displays.

Annual Western Montana Fair: August

Events at this annual fair include horse racing, a carnival, and fireworks.

Out to Lunch Festival: June–August

The Out to Lunch Festival is organized on the banks of the Clark Fork River each Wednesday in summer. This food and music festival has live entertainment. There are many food stalls where you can get lunch.

The Missoula community celebrates the Out to Lunch Festival.

Apply the Key Concepts

Key Concept 1 The location of a community has an effect on its economy and can help a community grow.

Activity

Draw a simple map of your state, and label the community where you live. Think of two natural resources in the community's location that helped its economy to grow, such as a river, mountains, or forests. Draw these features on your map, too.

New York City
Atlantic Ocean

Key Concept 2 Location influences a community's way of life.

Activity

Think about how the location of your community affects life there. What jobs does the location create? How does the location help people have fun? Draw four pictures showing jobs and activities that use the location of your community. Label your pictures.

Jobs in Shipping

Key Concept 3 Over time, communities change in some ways and stay the same in others.

Activity

Have a class discussion about the history of your community. Think of two or more examples of places or things that have changed in your community. Draw pictures showing the differences between the old and the new. Label your pictures.

Old   New

Create Your Own Travel Brochure

You have read the travel brochure about tourist attractions and activities in the city of Missoula. Now you are going to write your own travel brochure.

1. Study the Model

Look back at the description of travel brochures on page 20. Now read the brochure again. Notice how the teaser and the introduction attract the reader's attention and provide a general picture of the city. Read the body text of the brochure. Notice the headings used to organize the information. Note how the brochure gives facts and descriptive details that make the reader want to visit. Look at the photographs. Think about how the structure of the brochure helped you get familiar with the city.

Writing a Travel Brochure

◆ Choose a city for your travel brochure.

◆ Use a title and a teaser to capture attention.

◆ Write an introduction and then give details about the city under different headings.

◆ Use pictures with captions to show what the city looks like.

◆ Remember to include important facts about the city.

2. Choose a City

Now choose a city to write a travel brochure about. It should be a city that has many activities and attractions for tourists. You may find some ideas on the Internet or in books. You may want to choose a city that you have visited.

3. Research Your City

Now that you have chosen a city, you need to find more information about it. Use several different resources to find the information you need. Take notes as you come across important facts. Collect any photographs of the city that you can find. Organize your information under different headings such as Climate, What to See and Do, Tours, Sports Activities, Getting Around, and Where to Stay.

New York

1. Climate:

2. What to See and Do:

3.

4.

4. Write a Draft

Now write a draft of your travel brochure. First, write the title and the teaser. Give general information about the city, such as its location, in the introduction. Fill in details and facts under different headings. Be sure to use details and language that will persuade the reader to visit the city. Finally, write captions for the photographs you have collected.

5. Revise Your Draft

Read over what you have written. How clearly have you presented the information and photographs? Rewrite any unclear parts. Check your research to make sure that all the facts you have included are accurate. Correct any spelling or punctuation errors that you find.

Create Your Own Travel Review

Now that you have written your travel brochure, you can share what you have written with the class. With a group of students, you can compare and contrast different cities.

How to Write a Travel Review

1. Form a group.
Get together in a group of four students. Take time to read each other's travel brochures.

2. Take notes.
As you read each other's travel brochures, note down things that you like or dislike about the place described in the brochure. For example, you might like the outdoor activities of a place but not its climate.

3. Compare and contrast.
On another sheet of paper, compare and contrast the different cities. You can list them under headings such as *climate*, *location*, and *activities*.

4. Write a review.
Write a short paragraph explaining why you would or would not like to visit each of the places you have read about.

5. Share your travel reviews.
Put all the reviews at the front of the classroom. Take time to read all the travel brochures and reviews.

Glossary

businesses – shops or firms that people run to make money

community – a group of people living in an area

economy – the wealth that a community gets from its businesses

fertile – rich and good for growing crops

population – the number of people who live in a particular place

recreation – enjoyable activities that people do in their spare time

settlements – areas where groups of people have come and set up communities

tourism – all the businesses that service people who visit a place on vacation

trading post – a place where goods are bought and sold or exchanged

Index